CATHOLIC

Lent Devotional

2025

EMBRACING GRACE AND HOPE THROUGH THE
LENTEN SEASON

Arron Howard

Copyright © 2025 Arron Howard

All rights reserved. No part of this publication may be reproduced, distributed, or transmitted in any form or by any means, including photocopying, recording, or other electronic or mechanical methods, without the prior written permission of the publisher, except in the case of brief quotations embodied in critical reviews and certain other noncommercial uses permitted by copyright law.

Unless otherwise indicated all Scripture quotations are taken from the King James Version of the Bible.

CONTENTS

INTRODUCTION 6
WEEK 1: REPENTANCE AND TRUST IN GOD 10
   Day 1: Ash Wednesday Reflection 10
   Day 2: Thursday following Ash Wednesday 12
   Day 3: Friday following Ash Wednesday 14
   Day 4: Saturday following Ash Wednesday 15
   Day 5: First Sunday of Lent 16
   Day 6: Monday, Week 1 of Lent 17
   Day 7: Tuesday, Week 1 of Lent 18
   Day 8: Wednesday, Week 1 of Lent 19
   Day 9: Thursday, Week 1 of Lent 20
   Day 10: Friday, Week 1 of Lent 21
   Day 11: Saturday, Week 1 of Lent 22
   Day 12: First Saturday of Lent 23
WEEK 2: STRENGTH THROUGH FASTING 25
   Day 13: Second Sunday of Lent 25
   Day 14: Monday, Week 2 of Lent 27
   Day 15: Tuesday, Week 2 of Lent 28
   Day 16: Wednesday, Week 2 of Lent 29
   Day 17: Thursday, Week 2 of Lent 30
   Day 18: Friday, Week 2 of Lent 31
   Day 19: Saturday, Week 2 of Lent 32
WEEK 3: MERCY AND FORGIVENESS 33

Day 20: Third Sunday of Lent 33

Day 21: Monday, Week 3 of Lent 35

Day 22: Tuesday, Week 3 of Lent 36

Day 23: Wednesday, Week 3 of Lent 37

Day 24: Thursday, Week 3 of Lent 38

Day 25: Friday, Week 3 of Lent 39

Day 26: Saturday, Week 3 of Lent 40

WEEK 4: JOURNEYING WITH CHRIST'S PASSION 41

Day 27: Fourth Sunday of Lent 41

Day 28: Monday, Week 4 of Lent 43

Day 29: Tuesday, Week 4 of Lent 44

Day 30: Wednesday, Week 4 of Lent 45

Day 31: Thursday, Week 4 of Lent 46

Day 32: Friday, Week 4 of Lent 47

Day 33: Saturday, Week 4 of Lent 48

WEEK 5: HOPE IN SUFFERING 49

Day 34: Fifth Sunday of Lent 49

Day 35: Monday, Week 5 of Lent 51

Day 36: Tuesday, Week 5 of Lent 52

Day 37: Wednesday, Week 5 of Lent 53

Day 38: Thursday, Week 5 of Lent 54

Day 39: Friday, Week 5 of Lent 55

Day 40: Saturday, Week 5 of Lent 56

WEEK 6: TRIUMPH OF THE CROSS (HOLY WEEK) 57

    Palm Sunday: The King's Triumphal Entry 57

    Holy Thursday: The Institution of the Eucharist 59

    Good Friday: The Passion and Death of Jesus 60

    Holy Saturday: Waiting In Hope 61

ADDITIONAL FEATURES TO ENRICH YOUR LENTEN JOURNEY 62

    Prayers for Key Moments in Lent 62

MEDITATIONS AND GUIDED REFLECTIONS 65

    Meditation: The Garden of Gethsemane 65

    Meditation: The Seven Last Words of Christ 65

    Stations of the Cross: Simplified Reflections 66

PRACTICAL TIPS FOR LIVING LENT FULLY 71

INTRODUCTION

Purpose of the Devotional

Lent is a holy season in the Catholic tradition a time to break away from the distractions of everyday life and delve into a deeper connection with God. It is an invitation to partake in a spiritual journey highlighted by prayer, fasting, and almsgiving. These three foundations of Lent are not simple rituals but transforming acts that pull us closer to the heart of Christ.

Catholic Lent Devotional 2025: Embracing Grace and Hope Through the Lenten Season is created to be your companion along this journey. Each day, you will be led by:

Scripture Readings: These are founded in God's Word and reflect Lent's penitential and redemptive themes. Whether it's the call to repentance, the assurance of God's kindness, or the promise of redemption, each chapter has been carefully picked to connect strongly with your Lenten path.

Heartfelt Reflections: Lent encourages us to look upon the cross and appreciate Jesus Christ's enormous love and sacrifice. Through these insights, you will learn how His passion and resurrection intertwine with your everyday problems, pleasures, and ambitions.

Prayers: Each prayer is created to help you connect with God on a personal level, expressing your needs, and desires, and yearning for rejuvenation.

Actionable Challenges: These challenges are practical methods to carry out the Lenten invitation to conversion. Whether it's performing an act of kindness, blogging your appreciation, or fasting from personal comfort, each action is a chance to live the teachings of Christ.

The journey of Lent ends in the joy of Easter, a celebration of new life, redemption, and the triumph of grace over sin. This devotional will lead you through the seriousness of the season and help you prepare your heart to accept Easter's promise of renewal wholeheartedly.

Invitation to Commit

Embarking on a Lenten journey demands intentionality. This season is not merely a customary observance but a precious chance to get closer to God. To truly enjoy the spiritual richness of Lent, I ask you to make a commitment: set aside daily time for prayer, thought, and action.

Carve out a quiet area in your day to interact with this devotional. Whether it's early in the morning, during your lunch break, or before bed, let this time be sacred an undisturbed period when you may hear God's message and react with an open heart.

Start each session by requesting the Holy Spirit to lead you. As you read the Scripture texts, let the Word of God to speak to your heart. Let the meditations challenge and inspire you, pulling you into a deeper awareness of His grace. Offer the prayers with sincerity, knowing that God hears you and intends to act in your life.

Beyond your regular readings, take the challenges to heart. These are not simply responsibilities but chances to act out your faith in real ways. Whether it's forgiving someone who has wronged you, contributing to a charity organization, or fasting from something that distracts you from God, each challenge is a step toward being more like Christ.

Remember, Lent is a journey, not a sprint. There may be days when you struggle to be consistent, but don't allow discouragement stop you. God's mercy is sufficient, even in our frailty. Return to Him each day with a fresh resolve, knowing that He is always waiting to accept you.

This Lenten season is an invitation to change. By devoting yourself to this devotional, you are choosing to travel with Christ into the desert, to the crucifixion, and eventually to the empty tomb. Trust that this adventure will not leave you the same. It will strengthen your faith, rejuvenate your soul, and prepare your heart to completely enjoy the pleasure of Easter.

WEEK 1: REPENTANCE AND TRUST IN GOD

Day 1: Ash Wednesday Reflection

Scripture: "Therefore also now, saith the Lord, turn ye even to me with all your heart, and with fasting, and with weeping, and with mourning: And rend your heart, and not your garments, and turn unto the Lord your God: for he is gracious and merciful, slow to anger, and of great kindness, and repenteth him of the evil" (Joel 2:12-13 KJV).

Reflection: As we begin Lent, Ash Wednesday reminds us of our mortality: "You are dust, and to dust, you shall return." This sad fact encourages us to return to God and acknowledge the kindness and compassion that He has bestowed upon us. A public proclamation that we are prepared to align our hearts with God is represented by the ashes, which are a sign of repentance. It is not the external display that is important, but rather the change that occurs inside. So, how are you going to break your heart today?

Prayer: Lord, as I begin this Lenten journey, help me to seek You with all my heart. May the act of fasting and praying bring me closer to Jesus Christ. Transform me, Lord, from the inside out. Amen.

Action Challenge: Write down one area in your life where you feel estranged from God. Commit to giving it to Him in prayer and deed during Lent.

Day 2: Thursday following Ash Wednesday

Scripture: "I call heaven and earth to record this day against you, that I have set before you life and death, blessing and cursing: therefore choose life, that both thou and thy seed may live: That thou mayest love the Lord thy God, and that thou mayest obey his voice, and that thou mayest cleave unto him: for he is thy life, and the length of thy days: that thou mayest dwell in the land which the Lord sware unto thy fathers, to Abraham, to Isaac, and to Jacob, to give them" (Deuteronomy 30:19-20 KJV).

Reflection: God's call to choose life is not simply about physical existence it's about living completely in His grace. Lent is a time to assess our decisions and whether they bring us toward life in Christ or away from it. Choosing life requires turning away from sin, adopting His commands, and believing in His promises. Today, evaluate the minor decisions you make. Are they anchored in love, truth, and faith?

Prayer: Father, direct my heart to choose life in everything that I do. Help me to depart from sin and live faithfully in Your ways. Fill me with the confidence to believe in Your plan for my life. Amen.

Action Challenge: Identify one habit or action that does not accord with choosing life in Christ. Make a deliberate effort to replace it with something life-giving, such as prayer or a tiny act of compassion.

Day 3: Friday following Ash Wednesday

Scripture: "Is not this the fast that I have chosen? to loose the bands of wickedness, to undo the heavy burdens, and to let the oppressed go free, and that ye break every yoke? Is it not to deal thy bread to the hungry, and that thou bring the poor that are cast out to thy house? when thou seest the naked, that thou cover him; and that thou hide not thyself from thine own flesh?" (Isaiah 58:6-7 KJV).

Reflection: Fasting is more than refraining from eating; it's a spiritual practice in selflessness. Isaiah reminds us that authentic fasting connects our hearts with God's mission: caring for the downtrodden and breaking the bonds of injustice. How may your Lenten fasting transcend beyond personal sacrifice to become an act of love and justice for others?

Prayer: Lord, change my fasting into a sacrifice of love. Open my eyes to the needs of people around me, and grant me the strength to serve them with compassion and humility. Amen.

Action Challenge: Donate food, clothes, or resources to a local shelter or charity. If feasible, offer your time to help the needy in your community.

Day 4: Saturday following Ash Wednesday

Scripture: "Shew me thy ways, O Lord; teach me thy paths. Lead me in thy truth, and teach me: for thou art the God of my salvation; on thee do I wait all the day" (Psalm 25:4-5 KJV).

Reflection: As we begin our Lenten journey, Psalm 25 urges us to seek God as our guide. Life frequently seems like a tangle of options, temptations, and uncertainties. But through prayer and scripture, we may beg God to enlighten our way. Are you trusting God to lead your steps, or are you attempting to navigate alone?

Prayer: Heavenly Father, show me Your ways and teach me Your truth. May my hope always rest in You, even in times of uncertainty and suffering. Lead me on the road to holiness. Amen.

Action Challenge: Set aside 10 minutes today to think quietly on a tough choice or event in your life. Ask God for wisdom and listen for His instructions.

Day 5: First Sunday of Lent

Scripture: "Then was Jesus led up of the Spirit into the wilderness to be tempted of the devil. And when he had fasted forty days and forty nights, he was afterward an hungred" (Matthew 4:1-2 KJV).

Reflection: Jesus' stay in the desert offers the model for our Lenten journey. His fasting wasn't merely physical; it was a preparation for spiritual wars. In times of weakness, the adversary tempts us to depart from God's will. Yet Jesus reminds us that even amid hunger and difficulty, we can stay loyal. What temptations do you confront in your wilderness? How can you depend on God for strength?

Prayer: Lord Jesus, in my times of weakness and temptation, remind me of Your example in the desert. Strengthen me to choose loyalty above comfort. Amen.

Action Challenge: Identify a personal "wilderness" location in your life, where you feel most tempted or far from God. Commit to praying each day for strength in this area.

Day 6: Monday, Week 1 of Lent

Scripture: "And God saw their works, that they turned from their evil way; and God repented of the evil, that he had said that he would do unto them; and he did it not" (Jonah 3:10 KJV).

Reflection: The inhabitants of Nineveh repented with sincerity, and God granted them kindness. Lent is a reminder that no sin is too grave for God's forgiveness. His kindness is always accessible to those who turn to Him with contrite hearts. Today, think on an area of your life where you need His compassion. Remember, God's forgiveness is a gift waiting for you to receive.

Prayer: Merciful God, thank You for Your unlimited forgiveness. Help me to approach You with humility and move away from sin. Create in me a pure heart, O Lord. Amen.

Action Challenge: Spend a few time analyzing your conscience. If feasible, arrange a time for the Sacrament of Reconciliation this week.

Day 7: Tuesday, Week 1 of Lent

Scripture: "Lay not up for yourselves treasures upon earth, where moth and rust doth corrupt, and where thieves break through and steal: But lay up for yourselves treasures in heaven, where neither moth nor rust doth corrupt, and where thieves do not break through nor steal: For where your treasure is, there will your heart be also" (Matthew 6:19-21 KJV).

Reflection: Jesus invites us to evaluate our attachments. Are we focused on collecting money and goods, or are we working for spiritual riches? Lent challenges us to let go of worldly distractions and concentrate on cultivating a relationship with God. Consider: Where is your treasure? Is it in worldly luxuries, or in the everlasting delight of heaven?

Prayer: Lord, teach me to want the riches of heaven above everything else. Help me to let go of everything that draws my heart away from You. Let my emphasis be on Your kindness and grace. Amen.

Action Challenge: Choose one property or indulgence that you can live without this week. Donate it to someone in need or contribute the money you would have spent on it to a charity organization.

Day 8: Wednesday, Week 1 of Lent

Scripture: "Draw nigh to God, and he will draw nigh to you. Cleanse your hands, ye sinners; and purify your hearts, ye double minded" (James 4:8 KJV).

Reflection: Drawing closer to God demands a commitment to cleanse our hearts. James reminds us that repentance is more than simply words; it is an act of turning our entire selves toward God. Lent is the best opportunity to think on how you might develop your connection with Him. What measures can you take today to grow close to God?

Prayer: Father, I wish to come closer to You. Cleanse myself of everything that divides me from Your love. Help me to live in purity and honesty each day. Amen.

Action Challenge: Spend time in Eucharistic Adoration or in a peaceful area of prayer. Ask God to disclose one area in your life where He is encouraging you to get closer to Him.

Day 9: Thursday, Week 1 of Lent

Scripture: "And he said to them all, If any man will come after me, let him deny himself, and take up his cross daily, and follow me" (Luke 9:23 KJV).

Reflection: Following Jesus involves accepting the cross—not as a burden, but as a road to salvation. The crosses in our lives—struggles, sacrifices, and challenges—are chances to develop in faith and trust in God. How can you bear your cross today with love and persistence, knowing it draws you closer to Christ?

Prayer: Lord Jesus, assist me to accept the cross in my life. Teach me to bear it with humility and faith, knowing that it leads to unity with You. Amen.

Action Challenge: Identify one issue in your life and give it up to God as a prayer. Ask for His strength to bear it with grace and patience.

Day 10: Friday, Week 1 of Lent

Scripture: "Therefore if thou bring thy gift to the altar, and there rememberest that thy brother hath ought against thee; Leave there thy gift before the altar, and go thy way; first be reconciled to thy brother, and then come and offer thy gift" (Matthew 5:23-24 KJV).

Reflection: Reconciliation is a cornerstone of the Christian faith. Jesus warns us that we cannot truly commit ourselves to God if we are hanging onto grudges or unsolved issues. Lent is a time to seek peace with people, as well as with God. Is there someone you need to forgive or ask forgiveness from today?

Prayer: Lord, help me to be a peacemaker. Soften my heart to forgive those who have injured me and give me the strength to seek reconciliation with those I have offended. Amen.

Action Challenge: Take one tangible action toward reconciliation with someone in your life—send a message, make a call, or pray for them with an open heart.

Day 11: Saturday, Week 1 of Lent

Scripture: "The Lord is nigh unto them that are of a broken heart; and saveth such as be of a contrite spirit" (Psalm 34:18 KJV).

Reflection: God's presence is particularly close to people who are struggling. If you are bearing anguish or sorrow, remember that the Lord is your shelter and strength. Lent encourages us to entrust our brokenness to God, knowing that He can heal and restore us. Where do you need His healing touch today?

Prayer: Heavenly Father, thank You for being near to the brokenhearted. Bring healing to my wounds and restore my soul with Your compassion and kindness. Amen.

Action Challenge: Reach out to someone who may be feeling brokenhearted or overburdened. Offer a listening ear, a kind word, or a prayer for their recovery.

Day 12: First Saturday of Lent

Scripture: "I wait for the Lord, my soul doth wait, and in his word do I hope. My soul waiteth for the Lord more than they that watch for the morning: I say, more than they that watch for the morning" (Psalm 130:5-6 KJV).

Reflection: Waiting can be difficult, yet the psalmist reminds us that it is in waiting that we place our trust in God's timing and promises. Like the watchman who waits for the dawn, we are called to wait for the Lord with hope and expectation, knowing that His light will surely come. Lent is a season of waiting and preparing our hearts for the joy of Easter. How can you wait on the Lord with faith and patience today?

Prayer: Lord, in the moments of waiting, teach me to trust in You. Help me to place my hope in Your word and Your promises. May I find peace in the knowledge that Your timing is perfect and Your love never fails. Amen.

Action Challenge: Spend 15 minutes today in silent prayer or meditation, focusing on a scripture passage that reminds you of God's faithfulness. Write down any worries or desires that come to mind and offer them to the Lord, trusting in His perfect timing.

WEEK 2: STRENGTH THROUGH FASTING

The second week of Lent allows us to meditate on the spiritual value of fasting. Far beyond refraining from eating, fasting is a transforming practice that strengthens our dependence on God, purifies our hearts, and opens us to grace.

Day 13: Second Sunday of Lent

Scripture: "Moreover when ye fast, be not, as the hypocrites, of a sad countenance: for they disfigure their faces, that they may appear unto men to fast. Verily I say unto you, They have their reward. But thou, when thou fastest, anoint thine head, and wash thy face; That thou appear not unto men to fast, but unto thy Father which is in secret: and thy Father, which seeth in secret, shall reward thee openly" (Matthew 6:16-18 KJV).

Reflection: Fasting is not about appearances or outward affirmation; it is a secret gift to God. Jesus tells us to fast with humility and delight, seeking heavenly blessings rather than human applause. As you fast this Lent, consider how you may make fasting an act of love for God and others, done quietly and truly.

Prayer: Lord, enable me to fast with a glad and humble heart. Let my sacrifices be appealing to You and lead me closer to Your will. Amen.

Action Challenge: Choose a day this week for an intentional fast—whether from food, distractions, or habits. Use the time and energy saved to pray or aid someone in need.

Day 14: Monday, Week 2 of Lent

Scripture: "And if thou draw out thy soul to the hungry, and satisfy the afflicted soul; then shall thy light rise in obscurity, and thy darkness be as the noonday" (Isaiah 58:10 KJV).

Reflection: Fasting is a chance to shift emphasis from self to others. Isaiah asks us to utilize our fasting as a method to aid those in need, changing hunger into compassion. Consider how your sacrifices might benefit others. What can you give up today to bring light to someone else's darkness?

Prayer: Heavenly Father, use my fasting to help others and praise Your name. Help me to perceive the needs of others around me and react with compassion and kindness. Amen.

Action Challenge: Skip a lunch today and give the money you would have spent to a food bank or charity that feeds the needy.

Day 15: Tuesday, Week 2 of Lent

Scripture: "I know both how to be abased, and I know how to abound: every where and in all things I am instructed both to be full and to be hungry, both to abound and to suffer need. I can do all things through Christ which strengtheneth me" (Philippians 4:12-13 KJV).

Reflection: Fasting teaches us the key of contentment: dependence on God. Whether in prosperity or famine, we find strength not in worldly luxuries but in Christ's mercy. When hunger or sacrifice seems tough, remember that God supports you. How might fasting help you trust more profoundly in God's provision?

Prayer: Lord, teach me to depend on You in all situations. In times of hunger or weakness, help me find strength in Your love and grace. Amen.

Action Challenge: Reflect on an area of your life where you struggle with satisfaction. Pray for God's power to enable you accept His sufficiency.

Day 16: Wednesday, Week 2 of Lent

Scripture: "But he answered and said, It is written, Man shall not live by bread alone, but by every word that proceedeth out of the mouth of God" (Matthew 4:4 KJV).

Reflection: Jesus' answer to Satan in the desert reminds us that our ultimate need is not bodily but spiritual. Fasting shows the limits of worldly things and leads us to the sustenance of God's Word. When you experience the pains of hunger, turn your heart to Scripture and let it nourish your spirit.

Prayer: Lord Jesus, let my fasting remind me of my need for Your Word. May I thirst for Your truth more than for the things of this world. Amen.

Action Challenge: Spend 15 minutes reading and thinking on a favorite Bible verse. Reflect on how it nurtures your soul.

Day 17: Thursday, Week 2 of Lent

Scripture: "Casting all your care upon him; for he careth for you" (1 Peter 5:7 KJV).

Reflection: Fasting might bring suffering, but it also offers room for us to give our anxieties to God. By denying ourselves, we are reminded of our need on Him. Use your fasting today as a prayer of submission, placing your concerns on the One who loves you.

Prayer: Father, I offer You my fears and burdens. Help me to believe in Your care and find serenity in Your presence. Amen.

Action Challenge: Write down three fears or anxieties and give them to God in prayer. Trust Him to bear them for you.

Day 18: Friday, Week 2 of Lent

Scripture: "And Jesus said unto them, I am the bread of life: he that cometh to me shall never hunger; and he that believeth on me shall never thirst" (John 6:35 KJV).

Reflection: Fasting brings us to the actual Bread of Life, Jesus Christ. Physical hunger passes, but the nutrition of His presence is forever. As you fast today, remember that Jesus fills every yearning of your heart. How might you pursue Him more thoroughly today?

Prayer: Lord Jesus, You are the Bread of Life. Fill me with Your presence and fulfill my soul with Your love. Amen.

Action Challenge: Attend Mass or spend time in Eucharistic Adoration, thinking on Jesus as the Bread of Life.

Day 19: Saturday, Week 2 of Lent

Scripture: "Therefore also now, saith the Lord, turn ye even to me with all your heart, and with fasting, and with weeping, and with mourning" (Joel 2:12 KJV).

Reflection: Fasting is an act of returning to God with all our hearts. It is a physical representation of a spiritual yearning to be closer to Him. Use today to evaluate your heart. Is there anything you need to relinquish to truly return to God?

Prayer: Lord, I come back to You with all my heart. Accept my fasting as a demonstration of my love and devotion for You. Draw me closer to Your kindness and grace. Amen.

Action Challenge: Spend time in prayer asking God to disclose anything in your heart that needs to be relinquished. Write it down and commit to give it to Him.

WEEK 3: MERCY AND FORGIVENESS

In this third week of Lent, we shift our emphasis to God's unlimited compassion and His demand for us to give that kindness to others. As we reflect on the forgiveness we have received, we are asked to forgive others and to be agents of God's grace in the world.

Day 20: Third Sunday of Lent

Scripture: "Be ye therefore merciful, as your Father also is merciful" (Luke 6:36 KJV).

Reflection: Mercy is at the center of God's essence. Jesus encourages us to mirror that divine mercy in our own lives by forgiving others, demonstrating compassion, and extending love to those in need. Mercy originates in the heart and pours into action. How may you exemplify the kindness of God today?

Prayer: Father of Mercy, allow me to reflect Your love and compassion in my words and deeds. Teach me to be compassionate, just as You are kind to me. Amen.

Action Challenge: Perform a random act of kindness for someone today, demonstrating God's compassion in a practical manner.

Day 21: Monday, Week 3 of Lent

Scripture: "And be ye kind one to another, tenderhearted, forgiving one another, even as God for Christ's sake hath forgiven you" (Ephesians 4:32 KJV).

Reflection: Forgiveness is not always easy, but it is needed for healing and serenity. Just as we have been forgiven by Christ, we are required to forgive others. Letting rid of wrath and resentment frees our hearts to experience God's grace more completely. Who do you need to forgive today?

Prayer: Lord, grant me the strength to forgive as You have forgiven me. Soften my heart and fill it with compassion for those who have wronged me. Amen.

Action Challenge: Take a step toward forgiveness by praying for someone who has hurt you. Ask God to bless them and help you release any animosity.

Day 22: Tuesday, Week 3 of Lent

Scripture: "Who is a God like unto thee, that pardoneth iniquity, and passeth by the transgression of the remnant of his heritage? he retaineth not his anger for ever, because he delighteth in mercy" (Micah 7:18 KJV).

Reflection: God's joy in extending compassion reminds us that forgiveness is not a burden but a gift. He longs to heal our brokenness and bring us back into communication with Him. Reflect on the ways God has showed compassion to you. How can you offer such kindness to others?

Prayer: Merciful God, thank You for Your unending love and forgiveness. Teach me to pleasure in extending kindness to others, just as You delight in forgiving me. Amen.

Action Challenge: Write a letter of forgiveness to someone who has injured you, even if you don't send it. Offer the pain to God in prayer.

Day 23: Wednesday, Week 3 of Lent

Scripture: "Blessed are the merciful: for they shall obtain mercy" (Matthew 5:7 KJV).

Reflection: Mercy is a two-way street. As we demonstrate kindness to others, we open our hearts to accept God's mercy more fully. Being merciful involves choosing love over judgment, compassion over criticism, and forgiveness over animosity. How can you be a conduit of God's kindness today?

Prayer: Lord, assist me to live the Beatitudes by demonstrating kindness to others. Open my heart to both offer and accept Your compassion each day. Amen.

Action Challenge: Identify someone in your life who might need an encouraging word or a pleasant action. Reach out to them today.

Day 24: Thursday, Week 3 of Lent

Scripture: "As far as the east is from the west, so far hath he removed our transgressions from us" (Psalm 103:12 KJV).

Reflection: God's forgiveness is total and absolute. When we confess our sins, He takes them as far as the east is from the west, never to be held against us again. Do you believe in the completeness of God's forgiveness? Let go of any guilt or shame today, believing in His kindness.

Prayer: Lord, thank You for eliminating my sins and making me free. Help me to live in the pleasure and tranquility of Your forgiveness. Amen.

Action Challenge: Spend 5 minutes in quiet, thinking on God's forgiveness. If possible, plan to receive the Sacrament of Reconciliation this week.

Day 25: Friday, Week 3 of Lent

Scripture: "Then came Peter to him, and said, Lord, how oft shall my brother sin against me, and I forgive him? till seven times? Jesus saith unto him, I say not unto thee, Until seven times: but, Until seventy times seven" (Matthew 18:21-22 KJV).

Reflection: Forgiveness is not a one-time deed but a constant practice. Jesus' answer to Peter pushes us to let go of the scorecard and forgive without bounds. When we forgive repeatedly, we mirror God's infinite kindness. Is there someone you need to forgive again today?

Prayer: Lord Jesus, teach me to forgive without reckoning the cost. Help me to love as You love and to offer Your kindness to others eternally. Amen.

Action Challenge: Think about someone you have forgiven previously but still struggle with bitterness against. Pray for them and surrender any remaining pain to God.

Day 26: Saturday, Week 3 of Lent

Scripture: "Forbearing one another, and forgiving one another, if any man have a quarrel against any: even as Christ forgave you, so also do ye" (Colossians 3:13 KJV).

Reflection: Forgiveness needs patience and humility. Paul reminds us that forgiveness is a decision to endure with one another in love, even when it is tough. As you ponder on God's forgiveness, pray for the grace to forgive with the same compassion.

Prayer: Lord, thank You for bearing with me in my shortcomings and forgiving my transgressions. Grant me the grace to do the same for others with patience and love. Amen.

Action Challenge: Make a list of persons you need to forgive, even in minor ways. Pray over the list, asking God for the grace to forgive them totally.

WEEK 4: JOURNEYING WITH CHRIST'S PASSION

This week, we go beside Jesus as He marches toward Calvary. By focusing on His suffering, we expand our knowledge of His love and sacrifice for us, helping our hearts to develop in thankfulness and humility.

Day 27: Fourth Sunday of Lent

Scripture: "For God so loved the world, that he gave his only begotten Son, that whosoever believeth in him should not perish, but have everlasting life" (John 3:16 KJV).

Reflection: The Passion of Christ starts with the unfathomable love of God. His willingness to send His Son to suffer for our sins is the greatest manifestation of kindness and grace. As you contemplate on this famous scripture, examine the depth of God's love for you individually. How does His sacrifice motivate you to love Him and others more deeply?

Prayer: Heavenly Father, thank You for the gift of Your Son. Help me to realize the depth of Your love and to react with a heart full of thankfulness. Amen.

Action Challenge: Write a letter to God expressing your thankfulness for His love and sacrifice. Use it as a personal prayer of thankfulness.

Day 28: Monday, Week 4 of Lent

Scripture: "Surely he hath borne our griefs, and carried our sorrows: yet we did esteem him stricken, smitten of God, and afflicted. But he was wounded for our transgressions, he was bruised for our iniquities: the chastisement of our peace was upon him; and with his stripes we are healed" (Isaiah 53:4-5 KJV).

Reflection: Isaiah's prophesy of the Suffering Servant reminds us that Jesus suffered our anguish and sin out of love. Every wound He sustained was for our recovery. As you ponder on His Passion, consider how you might bring your wounds and sins to Him for healing and salvation.

Prayer: Lord Jesus, by Your wounds, I am healed. Thank You for bearing my sins and suffering for my sake. Teach me to give my anguish to You. Amen.

Action Challenge: Spend time in prayer, conveying a particular issue or concern to Jesus. Trust Him to bear it for you.

Day 29: Tuesday, Week 4 of Lent

Scripture: "And he went a little farther, and fell on his face, and prayed, saying, O my Father, if it be possible, let this cup pass from me: nevertheless not as I will, but as thou wilt" (Matthew 26:39 KJV).

Reflection: In the Garden of Gethsemane, Jesus experienced indescribable suffering yet gave His will to the Father. His prayer tells us that genuine strength comes from accepting God's will, even in the midst of hardship. What is God calling you to submit to Him today?

Prayer: Father, at times of anxiety and uncertainty, help me to believe in Your will. Give me the strength to follow where You lead, even when the route is rough. Amen.

Action Challenge: Identify an area in your life where you are struggling to trust God. Pray for the strength to submit it to Him totally.

Day 30: Wednesday, Week 4 of Lent

Scripture: "Then said Jesus, Father, forgive them; for they know not what they do. And they parted his raiment, and cast lots" (Luke 23:34 KJV).

Reflection: Even while He hung on the cross, Jesus gave forgiveness to His persecutors. His example tells us that kindness is bigger than vengeance and that forgiveness may win over hate. Who do you need to forgive, even if it seems undeserved?

Prayer: Lord Jesus, thank You for Your limitless kindness. Teach me to forgive like You forgave, even when it is tough. Fill my heart with Your compassion and love. Amen.

Action Challenge: Meditate about someone you find hard to forgive. Pray for God to soften your heart and give you the grace to forgive them.

Day 31: Thursday, Week 4 of Lent

Scripture: "After this, Jesus knowing that all things were now accomplished, that the scripture might be fulfilled, saith, I thirst. Now there was set a vessel full of vinegar: and they filled a spunge with vinegar, and put it upon hyssop, and put it to his mouth. When Jesus therefore had received the vinegar, he said, It is finished: and he bowed his head, and gave up the ghost" (John 19:28-30 KJV).

Reflection: In His dying moments, Jesus stated, "It is finished." This was not a scream of loss but of victory. He achieved the task of saving mankind via His sacrifice. What does Jesus' greatest act of love imply for your life? How can you react to His offer of salvation?

Prayer: Lord Jesus, thank You for concluding the work of my redemption. Help me to live in the light of Your love and to honor Your sacrifice in whatever I do. Amen.

Action Challenge: Spend time in silent thought today, honoring Jesus for His sacrifice. Write down one way you can live more completely for Him.

Day 32: Friday, Week 4 of Lent

Scripture: "And when the sixth hour was come, there was darkness over the whole land until the ninth hour. And at the ninth hour Jesus cried with a loud voice, saying, Eloi, Eloi, lama sabachthani? which is, being interpreted, My God, my God, why hast thou forsaken me?" (Mark 15:33-34 KJV).

Reflection: Jesus' lament from the cross indicates the intensity of His pain, both bodily and spiritual. Yet even at this time, He committed Himself to the Father. When we feel abandoned or overwhelmed, we may remember that Jesus totally knows our grief and is with us in every difficulty.

Prayer: Lord Jesus, thank You for journeying through the depths of sorrow for my sake. In my darkest times, enable me to believe that You are close. Amen.

Action Challenge: Light a candle and spend time contemplating on the cross. Reflect on how Jesus' suffering provides you strength in your own struggles.

Day 33: Saturday, Week 4 of Lent

Scripture: "I am crucified with Christ: nevertheless I live; yet not I, but Christ liveth in me: and the life which I now live in the flesh I live by the faith of the Son of God, who loved me, and gave himself for me" (Galatians 2:20 KJV).

Reflection: Paul's remarks remind us that Jesus' sacrifice is not merely a historical occurrence but a current reality in our lives. Through His Passion, we are changed and called to live by faith. How can you allow Christ dwell more completely in you today?

Prayer: Lord, thank You for offering Yourself for me. Help me to live each day with trust, allowing Your love to flow through me. Amen.

Action Challenge: Choose one area of your life where you can represent Christ more clearly. Commit to a tiny deed today that demonstrates His love.

WEEK 5: HOPE IN SUFFERING

In this fifth week of Lent, we focus on the redeeming power of suffering. Through Jesus' Passion, we learn that our hardships are not pointless but may lead to spiritual development, stronger trust, and hope in God's promises.

Day 34: Fifth Sunday of Lent

Scripture: "For I reckon that the sufferings of this present time are not worthy to be compared with the glory which shall be revealed in us" (Romans 8:18 KJV).

Reflection: Paul tells us that the troubles we suffer in this life are transient, and they pale in contrast to the everlasting pleasure that awaits us. Lent allows us to see suffering through the lens of hope, knowing that God is working all things for good. What obstacles are you experiencing today, and how can you submit them to God's plan?

Prayer: Lord, help me to perceive my challenges as chances to grow closer to You. Fill me with hope in

Your promises and confidence in Your ultimate purpose. Amen.

Action Challenge: Spend time journaling on a current obstacle or hardship. Write a prayer submitting it to God and praising Him for His future glory.

Day 35: Monday, Week 5 of Lent

Scripture: "And he said unto me, My grace is sufficient for thee: for my strength is made perfect in weakness. Most gladly therefore will I rather glory in my infirmities, that the power of Christ may rest upon me" (2 Corinthians 12:9 KJV).

Reflection: God's grace is most visible in our times of weakness. Paul's words remind us that it is not our strength but God's that sustains us. When you feel weak or overwhelmed, lean into His grace and believe that His might will carry you.

Prayer: Lord, thank You for Your grace that have been sustaining me. Help me to rely in Your strength, particularly in my times of weakness. Amen.

Action Challenge: Identify one area of weakness in your life and seek God to work through it. Reflect on how His grace has strengthened you in the past.

Day 36: Tuesday, Week 5 of Lent

Scripture: "The righteous cry, and the Lord heareth, and delivereth them out of all their troubles. The Lord is nigh unto them that are of a broken heart; and saveth such as be of a contrite spirit" (Psalm 34:17-18 KJV).

Reflection: God is close to people who are suffering. He hears our screams and pledges to rescue us. When we are brokenhearted, we may find solace in His presence and faith in His saving power. How can you come close to God today, even in the face of pain?

Prayer: Lord, thank You for being near to the brokenhearted. Comfort me in my troubles and remind me of Your rescuing love. Amen.

Action Challenge: Reach out to someone who may be brokenhearted or hurting. Offer a word of encouragement, a listening ear, or a prayer for them.

Day 37: Wednesday, Week 5 of Lent

Scripture: "But they that wait upon the Lord shall renew their strength; they shall mount up with wings as eagles; they shall run, and not be weary; and they shall walk, and not faint" (Isaiah 40:31 KJV).

Reflection: When we lay our faith in God, He renews our strength and supports us through life's hardships. Lent is a time to elevate our eyes to Him and believe that He will carry us through. Where in your life now do you need God's power?

Prayer: Lord, replenish my strength and fill me with hope in You. Help me to believe in Your promises and depend on Your strength each day. Amen.

Action Challenge: Take a walk or spend time in nature today, thinking on God's faithfulness and strength.

Day 38: Thursday, Week 5 of Lent

Scripture: "Be careful for nothing; but in every thing by prayer and supplication with thanksgiving let your requests be made known unto God. And the peace of God, which passeth all understanding, shall keep your hearts and minds through Christ Jesus" (Philippians 4:6-7 KJV).

Reflection: Anxiety frequently distorts our ability to perceive God's purpose, but Paul urges us to bring everything to Him in prayer. When we abandon our anxieties, God's peace floods our hearts and thoughts. What fears can you bring to Him today?

Prayer: Lord, I offer You my anxieties and fears. Fill me with Your peace that exceeds all understanding and preserve my heart in Christ Jesus. Amen.

Action Challenge: Write down three things that are giving you anxiety. Offer each one to God in prayer, asking for His peace to replace your anxieties.

Day 39: Friday, Week 5 of Lent

Scripture: "These things I have spoken unto you, that in me ye might have peace. In the world ye shall have tribulation: but be of good cheer; I have overcome the world" (John 16:33 KJV).

Reflection: Jesus tells us that although tribulation is inevitable, so is His triumph. Through His Passion and Resurrection, He has defeated sin and death. As we prepare for Holy Week, take comfort in His promise of peace and triumph. How can you embrace this hope in your own struggles?

Prayer: Lord Jesus, thank You for conquering the world. Help me to take heart in Your triumph and believe in Your serenity, even in the midst of hardship. Amen.

Action Challenge: Reflect on a particular difficulty or obstacle in your life. Pray for God to teach you how His triumph might bring peace and hope to your circumstances.

Day 40: Saturday, Week 5 of Lent

Scripture: "Wherefore seeing we also are compassed about with so great a cloud of witnesses, let us lay aside every weight, and the sin which doth so easily beset us, and let us run with patience the race that is set before us, Looking unto Jesus the author and finisher of our faith; who for the joy that was set before him endured the cross, despising the shame, and is set down at the right hand of the throne of God" (Hebrews 12:1-2 KJV).

Reflection: As we approach Holy Week, we are encouraged to concentrate our attention on Jesus. He suffered the crucifixion for the pleasure of our salvation. Our hope resides in His triumph and the prospect of everlasting life. How can you endure in faith, believing in the delight put before you?

Prayer: Lord Jesus, help me to concentrate my eyes on You and run the race with endurance. Fill me with hope in the joy of Your promises and the grandeur of Your Resurrection. Amen.

Action Challenge: Reflect on your Lenten journey thus far. Write down one area where you've gotten closer to God and one area you'd want to continue working on.

WEEK 6: TRIUMPH OF THE CROSS (HOLY WEEK)

Holy Week enables us to dive deeply into the Passion of Christ, dwelling on His final sacrifice and triumph over sin and death. Each day carries tremendous spiritual importance, culminating in the joy of the Resurrection.

Palm Sunday: The King's Triumphal Entry

Scripture: "And a very great multitude spread their garments in the way; others cut down branches from the trees, and strawed them in the way. And the multitudes that went before, and that followed, cried, saying, Hosanna to the son of David: Blessed is he that cometh in the name of the Lord; Hosanna in the highest" (Matthew 21:8-9 KJV).

Reflection: Palm Sunday recalls Jesus' victorious arrival into Jerusalem, when He is acclaimed as King. Yet the same throng that yells "Hosanna!" will shortly cry "Crucify Him!" This conflict between joy and betrayal parallels our own emotions. We embrace

Christ as King but frequently stumble in our resolve to follow Him. As you contemplate on Palm Sunday, consider: What areas of your life require deeper submission to His kingship?

Prayer: Lord Jesus, I embrace You as my King. Help me to commit my heart totally to You and follow You faithfully, even when the journey is tough. Amen.

Action Challenge: Create a symbolic "cloak" by writing down one item you need to lay at Jesus' feet. Place it at a prayer place or altar as a show of surrender.

Holy Thursday: The Institution of the Eucharist

Scripture: "If I then, your Lord and Master, have washed your feet; ye also ought to wash one another's feet. For I have given you an example, that ye should do as I have done to you" (John 13:14-15 KJV).

Reflection: Holy Thursday allows us to focus on two significant gifts: the Eucharist and the invitation to humble service. In washing the disciples' feet, Jesus shows self-giving love and humility. Through the Eucharist, He provides His real Body and Blood as sustenance for our journey. How do you act out the vocation to serve and to accept Christ with gratitude?

Prayer: Lord Jesus, thank You for the gift of the Eucharist and for teaching me how to love through humble service. Help me to serve others with a heart full of love and appreciation. Amen.

Action Challenge: Perform an act of service for someone in your life today, demonstrating Christ's love and humility. If possible, spend time in Eucharistic Adoration.

Good Friday: The Passion and Death of Jesus

Scripture: "When Jesus therefore had received the vinegar, he said, It is finished: and he bowed his head, and gave up the ghost" (John 19:30 KJV).

Reflection: Good Friday brings us to the foot of the cross, where we see the ultimate act of love and sacrifice. Jesus freely bore the weight of our sins to rescue us. As you focus on His Passion, ponder on the depth of His love for you. How can you react to His sacrifice with deeper love and devotion?

Prayer: Lord Jesus, thank You for Your sacrifice on the cross. Help me to shoulder my own crosses with trust and appreciation, knowing that You have redeemed me. Amen.

Action Challenge: Pray the Stations of the Cross or contemplate on the Seven Last Words of Jesus. Spend time in quiet, contemplating on the meaning of His Passion.

Holy Saturday: Waiting In Hope

Scripture: "And when Joseph had taken the body, he wrapped it in a clean linen cloth, And laid it in his own new tomb, which he had hewn out in the rock: and he rolled a great stone to the door of the sepulchre, and departed" (Matthew 27:59-60 KJV).

Reflection: Holy Saturday is a day of peaceful waiting. The disciples confronted the solitude of the tomb, straining to cling onto hope. We, too, endure seasons of waiting, when God's presence seems distant. Yet Holy Saturday reminds us that God is constantly at work, even in the solitude. How might you trust Him more thoroughly in times of waiting?

Prayer: Lord, amid the solitude of Holy Saturday, help me to wait with hope and confidence in Your promises. Help me to remember that even amid darkness, You are providing fresh life. Amen.

Action Challenge: Spend time in solitary prayer today, meditating on areas of your life where you are waiting for God to intervene. Offer them to Him with confidence and hope.

ADDITIONAL FEATURES TO ENRICH YOUR LENTEN JOURNEY

Here are some carefully selected prayers, hymns, meditations, and reflections to deepen the spiritual impact of your Lenten journey

Prayers for Key Moments in Lent

A Prayer of Repentance

Use this prayer during the first week of Lent or before the Sacrament of Reconciliation.

Heavenly Father,
I come before You with a contrite heart, knowing of my faults and failings.
Cleanse me with Your kindness and rejuvenate my soul.

Help me to follow in Your ways and seek You with all my heart.

Thank You for the gift of forgiveness through Your Son, Jesus Christ.
May I never take Your goodness for granted. Amen

A Prayer for Fasting

This prayer might complement Week 2, focused on fasting and self-denial.

Lord Jesus,
You fasted in the desert to become closer to the father and prepare for Your mission.
Help me to accept fasting as a route to holiness and a method to disconnect from worldly pleasures.
Strengthen me when I feel weak and urge me to come to You in prayer.
May my fasting not only cleanse my heart but also serve as a gift of love for others.
Amen.

A Prayer at the Foot of the Cross for Good Friday, or while contemplating on Jesus' Passion.

My Lord and my God,
As I kneel at the foot of Your cross, I am overwhelmed by the depth of Your love.
You bore my sins and suffered unspeakable anguish to offer me salvation.
Teach me to bear my own cross with humility and bravery, believing in Your plan for my life.

Thank You for the gift of redemption. May I live in a manner that respects Your sacrifice.
Amen.

A Prayer of Trust in Waiting for Holy Saturday, or amid personal problems with waiting and stillness.

Father of Hope,
In the profound solitude of Holy Saturday, I wait with desire for Your promises to be realized.
When I feel alone, tell me that You are always around, working in ways I cannot see.
Strengthen my faith and fill my heart with hope, knowing that Your resurrection provides fresh life.
Help me to trust in Your time and relax in Your serenity.
Amen.

MEDITATIONS AND GUIDED REFLECTIONS

Meditation: The Garden of Gethsemane

Put yourself in the scenario of Jesus praying in the garden.

"Imagine the silence of the night, broken only by the rustle of olive branches and the soft murmurs of Jesus' prayer. Feel the weight of His grief as He anticipates the pain to come. Picture Him kneeling on the chilly ground, His perspiration like droplets of blood. He prays, 'Not my will, but Yours be done.' As you sit with Him in the garden, what worries or burdens can you submit to His loving will?"

Meditation: The Seven Last Words of Christ

Ponder on one of Jesus' final remarks each day during Holy Week.

Examples:

"Father, forgive them, for they know not what they do."
Reflect on God's limitless kindness and your duty to forgive others.
"It is finished."
Consider what Jesus did for you via His sacrifice and how you might behave in response.

Stations of the Cross: Simplified Reflections

First Station: Jesus is Condemned to Death

Reflection: Lord Jesus, You accepted judgment without complaint, demonstrating us the road of humility and confidence in God's plan. Teach me to accept difficulties with grace, knowing You walk with me.

Prayer: Jesus, help me to believe in Your plan, even when I confront injustice or hardship. Amen.

Second Station: Jesus Carries His Cross

Reflection: Lord Jesus, You carried the heavy cross for my behalf. Help me to shoulder my own difficulties with trust, knowing they join me to You.

Prayer: Jesus, grant me strength to bear my crosses with love and endurance. Amen.

Third Station: Jesus Falls for the First Time

Reflection: Lord, Your first fall reminds me of my vulnerability. Yet You rose again, exhibiting the power of resilience. Help me to rise when I fall in sin or despair.

Prayer: Jesus, teach me to believe in Your power when I feel weak. Amen.

Fourth Station: Jesus Meets His Mother

Reflection: Mary, your presence gave Jesus strength. Teach me to be there for others in their pain, providing love and support as you did.

Prayer: Mother Mary, help me to be a source of comfort and compassion for others. Amen.

Fifth Station: Simon of Cyrene Helps Jesus Carry the Cross

Reflection: Lord, You accepted aid from Simon in Your helplessness. Teach me to accept aid with humility and to provide support to those who bear great loads.

Prayer: Jesus, make me a willing assistance to those in need. Amen.

Sixth Station: Veronica Wipes the Face of Jesus

Reflection: Lord, Veronica's tiny act of compassion gave You comfort. Teach me that even tiny acts of kindness may show Your face to others.

Prayer: Jesus, enable me to serve others with modest, loving gestures. Amen.

Seventh Station: Jesus Falls for the Second Time

Reflection: Lord, you fell again beneath the weight of the cross. Yet You endured for love of me. Help me to rise when I feel overwhelmed and continue to follow You.

Prayer: Jesus, grant me the fortitude to rise again when I fall. Amen.

Eighth Station: Jesus Meets the Women of Jerusalem

Reflection: Lord, even in Your suffering, You consoled the ladies who cried for You. Teach me to go past my own grief and be there for others in their problems.

Prayer: Jesus, open my heart to the needs of others around me. Amen.

Ninth Station: Jesus Falls for the Third Time

Reflection: Lord, Your third fall demonstrates the depth of Your tiredness, but You persevered to Calvary. Teach me to persist with faith, even when the road seems insurmountable.

Prayer: Jesus, give me the strength to keep going when I feel I can no longer go. Amen.

Tenth Station: Jesus is Stripped of His Garments

Reflection: Lord, You were stripped of all, humiliated and exposed. Teach me to let go of attachment to earthly things and trust in You alone.

Prayer: Jesus, assist me to separate from what does not bring me to You. Amen.

Eleventh Station: Jesus is Nailed on the Cross

Reflection: Lord, the nails held You to the cross, but it was Your love for me that kept You there. Help me to offer my own sufferings for love of You and others.

Prayer: Jesus, help me to endure my sorrow with patience and compassion. Amen.

Twelfth Station: Jesus Dies on the Cross

Reflection: Lord, you offered Your life for me, displaying the depth of Your love. Help me to live for You, believing in the power of Your sacrifice.
Prayer: Jesus, by Your death, grant me new life in You. Amen.

Thirteenth Station: Jesus is Taken Down from the Cross

Reflection: Lord, Your corpse was put in the arms of Your Mother. Teach me to trust Mary's intercession, knowing she is with me in my pain and tribulations.

Prayer: Mother Mary, take me in your arms and guide me to Your Son. Amen.

Fourteenth Station: Jesus is Laid in the Tomb

Reflection: Lord, the tomb was not the end but the beginning of fresh life. Teach me to believe in the promise of Your Resurrection when I feel buried by life's hardships.

Prayer: Jesus, fill me with hope in the promise of everlasting life. Amen.

PRACTICAL TIPS FOR LIVING LENT FULLY

Living Lent purposefully may enhance your spiritual path and help you accept the season's emphasis on prayer, fasting, and almsgiving. Here are comprehensive, practical ways to make Lent more meaningful:

1. Creating a Lenten Prayer Corner in Your Home Purpose: A designated prayer place develops a feeling of respect and makes it easier to maintain a regular prayer habit throughout Lent.

How to Create It:

❖ **Choose a Quiet Location:** Find a tranquil place in your house where you may pray without interruptions. This might be a tiny table, a shelf, or a unique chair.

❖ **Add a Crucifix or Cross:** Place a crucifix or a plain cross as the centerpiece, reminding you of Christ's sacrifice.

❖ **Include Sacred Images or Statues:** Add images of Jesus, Mary, or saints that inspire you, such as an image of the Sacred Heart or Our Lady of Sorrows.

❖ **Use a Candle:** A lighted candle represents Christ as the Light of the World. You may light it during your prayer time to create a spiritual ambiance. Incorporate a Bible: Place a Bible or a Lenten devotional in the prayer spot for convenient access during thoughts.

❖ **Personal Touches:** Include a diary for penning prayers, rosary beads, or a little basin of ashes to signify the penitential season.

❖ **Change Elements Weekly:** Consider adding symbols that represent each week's Lenten theme, such as a miniature crown of thorns, a purple cloth, or a palm branch during Holy Week.

Use It:

Dedicate at least 10 minutes everyday to sit in this location, study scripture, and pray. Use this space for personal or family prayer.

2. Writing a Gratitude Journal to Recognize God's Blessings

Purpose: Focusing on appreciation transforms your perspective, allowing you to appreciate God's benefits even during times of sacrifice and fasting.

How to Begin:

Choose a Journal: Select a notebook or diary particularly for Lent. Consider one with blank pages or questions for thought.

Set a Daily Time: Dedicate 5–10 minutes each evening or morning to reflect on your day.

Write Three Gratitudes: Each day, jot down at least three things you are thankful for. They may be as simple as a kind remark, a moment of tranquility, or the beauty of nature.

Connect Gratitude to Lent: Reflect on how God's blessings are influencing your Lenten experience. For example: "I'm grateful for the courage and strength to fast today."
"I'm thankful for the forgiveness I experienced in Confession."

End with a Prayer: After writing, say a little prayer of thankfulness. For example: Lord, thank You for the benefits You've provided me today. Help me to recognize Your hand at work in my life.
Long-Term Impact:

By the conclusion of Lent, you'll have a collection of blessings to dwell on, emphasizing how God has been present in your journey.

3. Performing a "Mercy Check-In" Each Evening Purpose: A "mercy check-in" lets you review your acts everyday, ensuring you carry out the duty to demonstrate love, forgiveness, and compassion.

How to Practice:

❖ **Set Aside 5 Minutes Before Bed:** Use a quiet opportunity to reflect on your encounters during the day.

❖ **Ask These Questions:**

Did I demonstrate love today?
Recall times when you provided compassion, charity, or assistance to someone.

Did I forgive someone today?
Reflect on whether you let go of resentment or extended forgiveness, even quietly.

Did I beg for forgiveness today?
Examine if you made an attempt to heal any strained relationships.

Did I do an act of mercy?
Consider if you assisted someone in need, provided a kind word, or prayed for someone.

❖ **Write It Down:** Keep a brief diary to track your replies. Note areas for progress and times you experience God's kindness working through you. Pray for Guidance:

❖ Close the check-in with a prayer. For example: Lord, thank You for the chances to express compassion and mercy today. Forgive me for the times I failed to reflect Your love. Grant me the grace to do more better tomorrow.

4. Commit to a Weekly Family Almsgiving Project
How: As a family, select a charity or cause to support each week. This might involve contributing food to a local pantry, crafting cards for the elderly, or helping at a shelter.

5. Make Fridays "Digital Fasting" Days
How: Fast from social media, TV, or non-essential phone usage on Fridays. Use the opportunity to study scripture, pray, or spend quality time with loved ones.

6. Practice "Silent Saturdays"
How: Dedicate part of your Saturday to silent meditation, reflecting Jesus' time in the tomb on Holy Saturday. Use this stillness to listen for God's voice in prayer.